VIPER RUM

ALSO BY MARY KARR

Abacus (1987)

The Devil's Tour (1993)

The Liars' Club (1995)

VIPER RUM

BY

MARY KARR

WITH THE AFTERWORD
"AGAINST DECORATION"

A NEW DIRECTIONS BOOK

ACKNOWLEDGMENTS
Grateful acknowledgments are made to the editors and publishers of the maga-
zines in which some of these poems originally appeared: "Four of the Horsemen,"
"Viper Rum," "The Wife of Jesus Speaks," "Belongings," and "County Fair" ap-
peared in *Parnassus;* "Hubris," "The Pallbearer," and "Revenge of the Ex-Mistress"
appeared in *The New Yorker;* "Beauty and the Shoe Sluts" appeared in *The Atlantic
Monthly;* "The Century's Worst Blizzard" and "The Patient" appeared in *Poetry.*
"Hubris" has also appeared in *The Norton Anthology of American Poetry.* For acknowl-
edgments for material quoted in "Against Decoration," please see page 78.

AUTHOR'S NOTE
I am grateful to Brooks Haxton for his example, his timely edits, and for the line I
stole from "Sanskrit at First Snowfall." New Directions gave me much help: James
Laughlin provided *hilaritas,* Barbara Epler edits, and Tim Davis viper-specific cover
art. Also, Herb Leibowitz of *Parnassus* patiently dragged "Against Decoration" and
several poems here through clarifying revisions. So did Allen Grossman. My Syra-
cuse University students taught me innumerable poetic lessons, specific thanks to
Joel Brouwer, Pam Greenberg, Abby McMillen, and Heidi Peppermint for all man-
ner of lent wisdom and assistance. I also appreciate the prizes from PEN and The
Texas Institute of Letters that bought me time, and a research grant from Syracuse
University's College of Arts and Sciences.

PUBLISHER'S NOTE
Special thanks are due to David Kirizian of the Department of Herpetology at the
American Museum of Natural History for his kindness in helping to arrange the
photograph of vipers.

Design by Sylvia Frezzolini Severance
First published as a New Directions Paperbook Original in 1998
Manufactured in the United States of America.
New Directions Books are printed on acid-free paper.
Published simultaneously in Canada by Penguin Books Canada Limited.

Library of Congress Cataloging-in-Publication Data:
Karr, Mary.
    Viper rum / by Mary Karr ; with the afterword "Against decoration."
        p. cm.
    ISBN 0-8112-1382-X (alk. paper)
    I. Title.
PS3561.A6929V56   1998
811'.54—dc21   97–47576
                                                                CIP

New Directions Books are published for James Laughlin
by New Directions Publishing Corporation
80 Eighth Avenue, New York 10011

for Dev Milburn
and Deb Larson

lux perpetua

Contents

But never met this Fellow
Attended, or alone
Without a tighter breathing
And Zero at the Bone—
                    Emily Dickinson
                    "A narrow Fellow in the Grass"

Do not, my friends, swim here: I like you
living. . . .
                    Thomas Lux
                    "Snake Lake"

VIPER RUM

VIPER RUM

All day we had run-ins with jungle snakes.
Above my canoe, a tiny vine serpent
like a single strand of luminous-green linguini

moved in a quick, muscular S from black orchid
to unripe mango to strangler fig.
Back at the lodge, a coral snake on the stucco floor

sent an old Girl Scout rhyme slantwise through my head:
"Red by yellow, kill a fellow.
Red by black, friend of Jack."

The waiter caught it in a Hellmann's mustard jar,
and we all stood around the bar
while it swayed hesitant behind the glass.

Once it curled back in on itself
the small knot of fear in my chest
unloosed. Over stew, the archaeologist

told how his friend surprised
in a ceremonial Mayan pot
the fer de lance or Tommygoff,

which never doesn't bite. "She made
a double tourniquet right off
and only lost the limb," he said.

Far off, a howler monkey pack started
the whiskey-throated roars
that maybe kept a jaguar back.

That's when the proprietress brought out the viper rum,
a gallon jug wide-mouthed enough
to fit inside the wrist-thick python

that circled there, flat-faced.
Shot glasses went round. The lid unscrewed
let out some whiff of Caribbean herb

that promised untold mystery unfolding in your head.
The python's lidless eyes were white, mouth
O-shaped, perfect for a cocktail straw, I thought.

Then naturally, I cast back to those last years
I drank, alone nights at the kitchen sink,
bathrobed, my head hatching snakes,

while my baby slept in his upstairs cage
and my marriage choked to death.
I should have wound up in a fetal coil

eyes scalded of sight, staring out
at the warped and vacant world.
What plucked me from that fate

can't yet be named, but I do reverence to it
every day. So with my untouched shot glass still
flipped upside down, I said goodnight. Outside,

the moon was a smoky disk, the path to my hut
loaded with white magnolia petals,
so every step sent out a fragrant mist

that wound up filling my circular
thatched hut—the flowers' flesh
got mashed in my boot soles.

My hammock cradled me in its knotted web.
All around a thousand radiant wings
were shimmering. The jungle hummed.

for Deb Larson

INCANT AGAINST SUICIDE

Buy neither gun nor blue-edged blade.
Avoid green rope, high windows, rat
poison, cobra pits, and the long vanishing point
of train tracks that draw you to horizon's razor.

Only this way will another day refine you. (Natural death's
no oxymoron) Your head's a bad neighborhood:
Don't go there alone, even if you have to stop
strangers to ask the way, and even if

spiders fall from your open mouth.
This talk's their only exit. How else
would their scramble from your skull

escape? You must make room first
that the holy spirits might enter. Empty
yourself of self, then kneel down to listen.

THE WIFE OF JESUS SPEAKS

Ours was the first inch of time.
The word passion hadn't yet been coined,
and I'd not yet watched my beloved

laid out to butchery and worshipped as a virgin, son
of a virgin even. This was before the Roman
bastards hammered his arms wide

as for some permanent embrace,
before the apostles paid me to lie
he never shuddered to death in my arms, I never

feasted on his flesh that now feeds
any open mouth, and inside me he never released
with a shudder the starry firmaments

and enough unborn creatures to fill an ark
all in a salty milk I nursed on.
His God gave us no child,

and even the books of salvation have not seen fit
to save me. Not the first woman
a great man denied knowing,

I said no back, for eternity.
With a rope slung over a tree branch,
I put my face inside a zero,

and with a single step clicked off
his beloved world's racket. Now my ghost head bends
sharp to one side, as if in permanent awe.

When he came down to hell and held out
that pale hand for rescue, I turned my back
(the snapped vertebra like a smashed pearl).

So my soul went unharrowed.
In these rosy caverns, you worship
what you want. I have chosen that time

in time's initial measure, history's
virgin parchment, when with his hard
stalk of flesh rocking inside me, I was unwrit.

Before me, I hold no other god.

THE LAST OF THE BROODING MISERABLES

Lord, you maybe know me best
by my odd laments: My friend
drew the garage door tight,
lay flat on the cold cement, then
sucked off the family muffler
to stop the voices in his head.
And Logan stabbed in a fight, and Coleman shot,
and the bright girl who pulled a blade
the width of her own soft throat,
and Tom from the virus and Dad
from drink—Lord, these many-headed
hurts I mind.

                        I study each death
hard that death not catch me
unprepared. For help I read Aurelius,
that Stoic emperor who composed
fine Meditations in his battle tent.

Surely he overheard at night
the surgeons chopping through
his wounded soldiers' bones
and shovels of earth flung down
on blue faces, and near dawn,
the barbarian horses athunder.

Still, he judged the young man's death
no worse than the old's: each losing
just one breath. I would have waded
the death pits wailing
till I ruined good boots with lime—
a vulture for my dead too long,
or half a corpse myself.

Lord, let me enter now
your world, my face,

dip deep in the gloves
of these hands formed
to sow or reap or stroke
a living face. Let me rise

to your unfamiliar light,
love, without which the dying
wouldn't bother me one whit.

Please, if you will, bless also
this thick head I finally bow. In thanks.

for James Laughlin

FOUR OF THE HORSEMEN (HYPERTENSE AND STROKE, CORONARY OCCLUSION AND CEREBRAL INSULT)

Mother's on the sofa with her channel-changer raised,
aimed like a wrist-rocket at the last reality
she can alter. Her bearing's still imperial,

but each day she fades a little. Last winter a surgeon
reamed her heart out. He cut her leg from instep
to crotch for a vein, which left an inch-deep trench

I swabbed each day, then packed
with strips of medical gauze that looked like worms.
Lord God, it's sorry work.

She'd whimper *stop*, too frail
to pull away. Sometimes I sensed a presence
slinking the room's unlit perimeter. Its scaly tail

dragged shadows. More to the point, though,
Death lodged in her rib cage,
which they'd pried open. Actual staples

held halves of my mother's chest
fast to the scarlet scalpel line.
Such meat hunks we are, such heavy corpses

born up by frail breath, as Epictetus said
according to Heraclitus, for some dim wisdom
does filter down. Tell that to Mother, though,

on the sofa chain-smoking *Mores*. She scorns
delivered wisdom: Ashtrays stud the room,
so unsquashed cigarettes she forgot she lit

send up curls of smoke like altar offerings,
steam from the entrails of sacred butchered birds.
Please don't die, I say. She rolls her eyes.

Once when she was sleeping I pressed my ear
to her bony chest as if to power up
that sluggish beat a bit. Instead I heard

the horsemen she prays to—not riding out at a lope
with silk capes blown back, but at a slow plod,
bent over their saddle horns like tired commas,

animals unspurred, only coming at her behest.

HUBRIS

The man in the next office
was born a dwarf.
Mornings, when we wait
for the elevator, he quotes Whitman,
while I shamelessly covet
his gray baseball jacket.
Maybe he doesn't mean
to be a figure of courage
with his cane and his corkscrew knee,
this smart man who can't reach
some sinks. No doubt he'd like
to take the stairs like me,
two at a pop. Instead,
as the elevator numbers fail
to fall to us fast enough,
he waves me on—It'll come
eventually, he says with cheer.
He grows ever smaller
in the stairwell. I ascend.

THE PATIENT

At the end we prayed for death,
even phoned funeral homes
from his room for the best
cremation deal. But back
when he was tall, he once put
my ailing cat to sleep,
or helped the vet and me
hold it flat to the table
while we felt all muscles
tighten for escape
then freeze that way. Later
in my father's truck,
I held the heavy shoebox on my lap.
He said, I ever git like that
you do the same. I remember the slight
weight of my ten-year-old head
nodding without a pause. We peeled
from the gravel lot onto the rain-
blurred road. What did I know
of patience then? Or my dad
for that matter, shifting gears.
Each white second was knit
into a sheet that settled over his features
like a snowfield. Forgive me,
Father, this terrible face.
I was the patient one.
I got what I wanted.

ADIEU

In the soapy water our bodies steamed
like newborns still flushed from the womb's caul.
This bath was our farewell ritual: We'd played

Hide the Soap and Tropical Rain Forest.
In the fogged mirror our forms
had merged and come untwined.

The clock ticked down to my dawn flight,
but this time a vow had been spoken,
a bond entered into, unwitnessed

by any assembly, but nonetheless
sacred. The ring on my hand shone
with the firmament's starlight. Though candles around us

guttered and the water cooled and each cupped
the other's face with withered hands, our bodies
steamed, our tired souls could not stop rising.

for Peter

BEAUTY AND THE SHOE SLUTS

Mother kneels at her closet of dancing shoes
to see which ones I fit—sherbet green
taffeta and crimson crocodile, pumps

in Easter pink, plus a dozen black heels
with bows or aglisten with rhinestones,
all wicked run down. Likewise,

she's gnarled as a tree root, her spine's
warped her shorter than me, over whom
she once towered with red hair

brushed back into flame points.
Seeing her handle those scarred leather hides, I quote
the maenads' sad lament from *The Bacchae*.

After they've chased down
the fleeing god, fucked him dead, sucked
all flesh from his bones, dawn spills light

on their blood-sticky mouths,
and it's like every party you ever stayed
too late at. In chorus they sing and grieve:

"Will they come to me ever again,
the long, long dances?"
And Mother holding a black patent ankle strap

like a shackle on a spike heel
(it must've been teetering hell to wear) glances
sidewise from her cloudy hazel eyes and says, "No,

praise God and menopause, they won't."

FIELD OF SKULLS

Stare hard enough at the fabric of night,
and if you're predisposed to dark—let's say
the window you've picked is a black
postage stamp you spend hours at,
sleepless, drinking gin after the *I Love
Lucy* reruns have gone off—stare

like your eyes have force, and behind
any night's taut scrim will come the forms
you expect pressing from the other side.
For you: a field of skulls, angled jaws
and eye-sockets, a zillion scooped-out crania.
They're plain once you think to look.

You know such fields exist, for criminals
roam your very block, and even history lists
monsters like Adolf and Uncle Joe
who stalk the earth's orb, plus minor baby-eaters
unidentified, probably in your very midst. Perhaps
that disgruntled mail clerk from your job

has already scratched your name on a bullet—that's him
rustling in the azaleas. You caress the thought,
for it proves there's no better spot for you
than here, your square-yard of chintz sofa, hearing
the bad news piped steady from your head. The night
is black. You stare and furious stare,

confident there are no gods out there. In this way,
you're blind to your own eye's intricate machine
and to the light it sees by, to the luck of birth and all
your remembered loves. If the skulls are there—
let's say they do press toward you
against night's scrim—could they not stare

with slack-jawed envy at the fine flesh
that covers your scalp, the numbered hairs,
at the force your hands hold?

SUMMONS (OR THIS WON'T HURT YOU A BIT, AND IT'LL CHEER ME UP)

For an instant I looked away, and an ocean
blossomed between us, 3000 miles
of wild silk rippling. On the other side

your unreachable body. Listen,
the globe's meridians bore me,
and I deplore time zones and the lone heart's

metronome without your broad chest
thumping close counterpoint. No breath I draw
will properly fill my lungs till your fine spirit

again issues into me. No eyes will level pierce
this heart's core till your gaze again
sends the deep arrows flying. Darling,

remember: our faces in proximity make
a pure small space—a vessel or goblet
that could hold the whole Atlantic. Always

I stare you-ward: come spill yourself in me.

REQUIEM FOR THE NEW YEAR

On this first dark day of the year
    my daddy was born lo
these eighty-six years ago who now
    has not drawn breath or held
bodily mass for some ten years and still
    I have not got used to it.
My mind can still form to that chair him
    whom no chair holds.
Each year on this night on the brink
    of new circumference I stand and gaze
towards him, while roads careen with drunks,
    and my dad who drank himself
away cannot be found. Daddy, I'm halfway
    to death myself. The millenium
hurtles towards me, and the boy I bore
    who bears your fire in his limbs
follows in my wake. Why can you not be
    reborn all tall to me? If I raise my arms
here in the blind dark, why can you not
    reach down now to hoist me up?
This heavy carcass I derive from yours is
    tutelage of love, and yet each year
though older another notch I still cannot stand
    to reach you, or to emigrate
from the monolithic shadow you left.

THE GRAND MIRACLE

Jesus wound up with his body nailed to a tree—
a torment he practically begged for,
or at least did nothing to stop. Pilate

watched the crowd go thumbs down
and weary, signed the order.
So centurions laid Jesus flat

on a long beam, arms run along the crosspiece.
In each palm a long spike was centered,
a stone chosen to drive it. (Skin

tears; the bones start to split.)
Once the cross got propped up,
the body hung heavy, a carcass—

in carne, the Latin poets say, in meat.
(—The breastbone a ship's prow . . .)
At the end the man cried out

as men cry. (Tears that fill the eyes
grow dark drop and by drop: One
cries out.) On the third day,

the stone rolled back, to reveal
no corpse. History is rife
with such hoaxes. (Look at Herodotus.)

As to whether he multiplied
loaves and fishes, that's common enough.
Poke seed-corn in a hole and see if more corn

doesn't grow. Two fish in a pond
make more fishes. The altar of reason
supports such extravagance. (I don't even know

how electricity works, but put trust
in light switches.) And the prospect
of love cheers me up, as gospel.

That some creator might strap on
an animal mask to travel our path between birth
and ignominious death—now that

makes me less lonely. And the rising up
at the end into glory—the white circle of bread
on the meat of each tongue that God

might enter us. For 2000-near years
my tribe has lined up at various altars,
so dumbly I open this mouth for bread and song.

for John Holohan

MR. D. REFUSES THE BLESSING

He wanted to unscrew and reorder
the stars to guide his lost beloveds back.
Instead, he shook his fist at heaven.
And like one of those willful boneheads
who backs a swiveling truck
wildly the wrong way up the road,
he reversed himself against all flows.
To what should he bow his head, which said
it was smartest of all? On the tall
library ladder, he pulled down first one
heavy tome then another, but no book
ever raised him an inch. He did not wish
to be lifted but to climb himself;
not to receive grace, but to shape it
in his own clawed and hairy hands.
Hence he died high in the stacks,
his hand cobwebbed to the mystery shelf . . .

TERMINUS

She'd prayed her whole life to be a vessel
then became one: in her womb
a stray grub was rooting.

But practicality intervened (lack
of money, lack of man, interminable
love lack). So she donned a slit-backed robe.

The table she slid on rattled with parchment, as if
at procedure's end some unrolled scroll
might be issued. The trash bin was flesh-colored;

its bright orange decal read DANGER, the one word
in that unlit room till across the green backdrop
attendants came. Then it was *please* and *there* and

discomfort. The speculum warmed with tap water
was greased to fit her cunt. The mask strapped
to her face promised forgetting (breath of solvent),

till a pinch at her core augered truer (sharp cramp, bear
down, pressure). A sucking noise threatened
to inside out her whole self, but only swept out

the soulless (say it) thing she meant
and did not mean to bear. Not sin, I swear,
but bitter hurt she carried out the clinic door

to find a line of picketers and placards
nailed to broomsticks, and blind sun
she could not blink away.

LIMBO: ALTERED STATES

No sooner does the plane angle up
than I cork off to dream a bomb blast:
A fireball roiling through the cabin in slo-mo,
seat blown loose from its bolts,
I hang weightless a nanosecond
        in blue space

then jerk awake to ordered rows.
And there's the silver liquor cart jangling
its thousand bells, the perfect doses
of juniper gin and oak-flavored scotch
        held by a rose-nailed hand.

I don't miss drinking, don't miss
driving into shit with more molecular density
than myself, nor the *Mission Impossible*
reruns I sat before, nor the dead
space inside only alcohol could fill and then
        not even. But I miss

the aftermath, the pure simplicity:
mouth parched, head hissing static.
How little I asked of myself then—to suck
the next breath, suffer the next heave, live
till cocktail hour when I could mix
        the next sickness.

I locked the bathroom door, sat
on the closed commode, shirtless,
in filmy underpants telling myself that death
could fit my grasp and be staved off
while in the smeary shaving glass,
I practiced the stillness of a soul
        awaiting birth.

For the *real* that swarmed beyond the door
I was pure scorn, dead center of my stone and starless
universe, orbited by no one. Novitiate obliterate, Saint
Absence, Duchess of Naught . . .
A stinging ether folded me in mist.

Sometimes landing the head's pressure's enormous.
When my plane tilts down, houses grow large, streets
lose their clear geometry. The leafy earth soon fills my portal,
and in the gray graveyard of cars, a stick figure
becomes my son in royal blue cap flapping his arms
as if to rise. Thank god for our place
in this forest of forms, for the *gravitas*
that draws me back to him, and for how lightly
        lightly I touch down.

THE PALLBEARER

The coffin I bore swung between us
like a battering ram against the door to heaven.
My friend was heavy carried by handles.

I listed. The plod was slow (no dirge).
The cherrywood cover got pittered with rain,
glossy with swirls in the grain

as with great red rivers risen to flood.
I too was flooded. My eyes brimmed
the green world blurry, though my face stayed flat.

The rhythm of walking took all my thought.
Later the shovels of dirt fell splat
on that cover, and they left a nice mound

like the start of a rose garden.
When I stretched on my narrow bed that night
I almost felt the strong hands heave me up;

my body swung through the dark like a child's.

for John Engman

THE CENTURY'S WORST BLIZZARD

We'd been holed up with the power cut
for days when the streetplow thundered past
shoving up a wall of ice that blocked my drive

and ultimately crumpled my cheap shovel
like an accordion. After that
the black phone rang: Judith's

cancer diagnosis, not just breast
but liver, and the very
marrow of her bones. Her voice

was calm. She wasn't coming back,
which fact she stated so plainly
I wrote it on the yellow

sticky note, where my pen had poised
to jot some errand I could run. Sharp
as a blade, Judith, 44,

and heretofore symptomless.
On the wire between us, distance
seemed to hiss. My son shrieked past,

silk Dracula cape flapping. Judith said
it sounded like I had to go.
She only wanted mail, instructing

not how to live, but why,
despite the pain, she should.
So all day I stared at the gray screen

of the battery-run laptop
the university where we teach had bought.
Yet the words on the snow screen

were black and patternless, flies
and gnats. Next morning, I scribbled
something dopey on a card.

I planned to wade to the snowy lump
of mailbox down the block,
and flung the front door wide.

But while we'd slept, icicles
had been growing from the eaves.
I faced a wall of them my height,

as if I'd been eaten by some giant beast
and stood encased in its mouth
and could only catch brief

slivers of the world between
its dripping teeth. Across the street
were other houses, other doors

gone vague behind other
glistening columns of ice.
My ancient neighbor chopped

inside his frozen cage with a pickaxe,
his body warped and bent.
Seeing me, he paused to tug his mitten off.

Then his pale fist—arthritic, curled
like a claw—came poking out.
He made an upward screwing motion,

which gesture caused a thundering
avalanche from his roof,
though the old man dodged

past it, miraculously untouched.
Of course he sank chest-deep in snow.
The domed sky was bitter blue, the wind

was sharp. Of course
the cancer cells in Judith's bones
still multiplied with exponential speed,

and the stamped card I held
said nothing smart except Hold on,
and the narrow road

I hoped to reach snaked by
like a river of glassy fire.
Nonetheless, I plunged

dumbly forward, wished hard
for a white mail truck, and just then,
from nowhere, one came puttering up.

REVENGE OF THE EX-MISTRESS

Dear X—
Finally met your wife
in Beef and Beer.
She hates it that you let me
pierce your ear, and time
you lost to me she guessed.
Still, we fell in love.
Please send her clothes
to my address. Best
wishes, no regrets—Another X.

DEAD DRUNK (OR THE MONSTER-MAKER AT WORK)

When Tom passed out in the snow
and blowing wind behind the bar,
he was flushed by spirits from solar
plexus to extremities.

But once the surgeon sawed away
his frost-black hands and feet,
Tom could no longer stand
himself, nor hold a doorknob,
nor, when lonely, fondle his lower parts.

He sat in the dayroom reading sports
(four stumps and an awful cough).
Custodians mopped a bull's eye round his chair,
or gave him lights, while a psychotic
tracked the flight of a winged skull
around the ward's perimeter. Sometimes
Tom felt his phantom hands appear
folded in his lap as if poured
from liquid fire, fingers locked in prayer.
Then he'd ask for Halcion, and sleep.

Released, let loose, back on the street, Tom begged enough
to keep a pint between his knees,
but finally couldn't draw sufficient
ethyl alcohol inside to meet
his nervous system's screaming needs.
Then he began to scream. A medic came
and knelt there on the street and didn't mind
Tom's pants were wet. This
was all the grace there was, unless you count
the patient janitor who once stubbed his smokes,
other maniacs who cut his meat, the coroner
who shook her head and said, *Please God*, above the corpse.
And you, dear reader. If you drove past

Tom's original post in snow, you might have stopped
and heaved him up all whole. That tale's
unwrit: We cannot make it so. This wheeling,
juniper-scented universe took him to sleep in blue ether.
So let us stand in company and grieve that fact:
Hail, Tom, asleep under snowflakes,
slack-jawed in burning cold.

ANIMISTIC ANATOMY

My student points out that we're dark
   in our bodies, which troubles me.
Somehow I always thought myself lit up
   like the transparent model from biology
with brightly dyed guts folded neat, brown
   liver, brain white as a slug. In physiology
I learned the twelve cranial nerves and how
   the eye upside-downs everything,
the broad rivers of the heart. Now I know
   my pupil admits for the whole world
just one pinprick of light, one recumbent picture
   of pen and lined paper. No homunculus
heaves a lever to hoist this hand to my brow.
   I only shine inside at death,
when the undertaker's whirling saw at last
   opens me to cold light. He'll be ignorant
to the soul which will rise
   in fiery mist. He will not heave it
with other organs on the scale, though the now
   dark parts of me will grow luminous
in his gloved hands. How I long to be opened
   and laid bare this way, weighed and measured,
illumined, my soul at last uncaged from ribs, rising.

for Abby McMillen

MALL CRAWL

I went to worship at the cathedral
of emptiness. The air was cool as mint.
Before me in the infant boat

my son fought with his covers.
Like some powdery-winged moth,
he longed to unfurl himself.

But the cotton batting I'd wound him in
held. The world that slid by his portal
was all white and right angles. I was a line mouth

and pin-dot eyes that sometimes loomed close.
When we mounted the black pedestrian belt
faces came gliding toward us—pale and blank,

bloated dolls from the factory line.
The elevator we wedged into became a jar
of steel and glass where we sucked

for air like insects through forkholes
the giant was kind enough to poke. We came
to spend ourselves and left wanting.

CHRIST'S PASSION

Sure we're trained to his suffering, sure
the nine-inch nails, and so forth.
And the cross raised up invoked

the body's weight so each wound tore,
and from his abdomen a length of gut
dangled down, longing towards earth.

He was a god, after all.
An eternal light swarmed in his rib cage
no less strong than the weaving nebulae that haul

this dirt-speck planet through its course.
Surely his flesh mattered less somehow, less
than yours to you. He hung against steel rods

with his whole being, and though the pain
was very pure, he only cried out once.
All that was writ down. But what if his flesh

felt more than ours, knew each breath
was a gift, and thus saw
beyond each instant into all others.

So a morsel of bread conjured up
the undulating field of wheat from whence it came,
and the farmer's back muscles

growing specific under his shirt
and the sad, resigned pace of the mule
whose opinion no one sought.

Think of all we don't see
in an instant. Cage that in one skull.
If Christ saw in each

pair of terrified eyes he met
every creature's gauzy soul
then he must have looked down from that bare hill

and watched the tapestry teem
till that poor carcass he borrowed
wept tears of real blood before they

unhooked it and oiled it and bound it
round with linen and hid it under a stone,
to rise again or not, I can only hope.

for Walt Mink

DOMESTIC RUINS

In a few mornings no man will shave in my mirror,
so I lie in misery's bed and savor that penultimate music:
Razor scrape and the splash of water.

After, fine black hairs ring the basin.
I stand here as if to decode them
like a gypsy girl with her oracle of tea leaves.

Still I know no more why we fail
than I did last night with moonlight on my back
while he entered me from behind

and the pure faceless weight
of our day's pain had us both bent
halfwise to near breaking.

How can I marry that?
In a few mornings no man
will shave his beloved face in the mirror.

What then will I stare back at? what toward?

THE INVENTION OF GOD IN A MOUTHFUL OF MILK

As the violin's body shudders with the tree's
   lost song, so my mother's soul longs
to rise from its fleshy husk. "I'm over this shit,"
   she says. Her gray eyes have sunk
to the sockets' hollows. (Beloved worlds)
   The concerto moans from the stereo,
and bare trees claw the sky. Surely hers was the first face
   I saw clear from the infant mist,
the whiskey timbre of her voice the first.
   My mouth was clamped to her breast.
Warm milk poured down my throat,
   and inside that lavender ether
I was a god afloat and barely came to sense
   an alternate god: Ma and ma and mama . . .

COUNTY FAIR

On the mudroad of plodding American bodies,
        my son wove like an antelope from stall
to stall and want to want. I no'ed it all: the wind-up
        killer robot and winged alien; knives
hierarchical in a glass case; the blow-up vinyl wolf
        bobbing from a pilgrim's staff.
Lured as I was by the bar-b-que's black smoke,
        I got in line. A hog carcass,
blistered pink on a spit, made its agonized slow roll,
        a metaphor, I thought, for anyone
ahead of me—the pasty-faced and broad. I half-longed
        for the titanium blade I'd just seen
curved like a falcon's claw. Some truth wanted cutting
        in my neighbors' impermanent flesh.
Or so my poisoned soul announced, as if scorn
        for the body politic
weren't some outward form of inner scorn,
        as if I were fit judge.
Lucky my son found the bumper cars. Once I'd hoped
        only to stand tall enough
to drive my own. Now when the master switch got thrown
        and sparks skittered overhead
in a lightning web, I felt like Frankenstein or some
        newly powered monster.
Plus the floor was glossy as ice. Even rammed head-on,
        the rubber bumper bounced you off unhurt
and into other folks who didn't mind the jolt, whose faces
        all broke smiles, in fact,
till the perfect figure-eight I'd started out to execute
        became itself an interruption. One face
after another wheeled shining at me from the dark,
        each bearing the weight of a whole self.
What pure vessels we are, I thought, once our skulls
        shut up their nasty talk.
We drove home past corn at full tassel, colossal silos,
        a windmill sentinel. Summer was starting.

My son's body slumped like a grain sack against mine.
            My chest was all thunder.
On the purple sky in rear view, fireworks unpacked—silver
            chrysanthemum, another in fuchsia,
then plum. Each staccato boom shook the night. My son
            jerked in his sleep. I prayed hard to keep
the frail peace we hurtled through, to want no more
            than what we had. The road
rushed under us. Our lush planet heaved toward day.
            Inside my hand's flesh,
anybody's skeleton gripped the wheel.

BELONGINGS

How deflated your sweaters looked in that final box,
all those empty sleeves criss-crossed over vacant chests,
a stack of metaphorical corpses.
When I pressed them down to squeeze out
that last inch of air, to compact the parcel (so much
      to ship back) stale camphor

fumed up like the sigh of someone
I'd failed to revive. *Give me
your breath,* you'd say, and I'd exhale
down your lungs. Long mornings in bed we'd lie
(my head on your chest) stare out the plate glass where leaves
      bloomed and started to blaze,

fell. Now alone nights, I often think
of those sweaters launched between shores
as our unborn, rocked in some ship's dank hold,
the box perhaps crawled on by rats,
misnumbered on the wide night's manifest,
      which endlessly scrolls its black

past my sight. My eyes sting. It's late.
Of the parcels for various loves
I've shipped, mourned, and soon
forgot, yours weighed most, cost most, went
deepest from the dark of me. I miss you
      my pole star.

Our very constellations are drowning.

LIFECYCLE STAIRMASTER

I have to fly all day to reach my home
        state, my sister's marble-floored house
                kept cool as a tomb in Texas heat.

Mired in my traveled-out flesh, I mount
        her stairmaster and sink floorward.
                Its tiny screens stay black

till I punch in age (40) and a weight
        no worse than college. The program I pick
                is *hill,* which consonates with *hell.*

If Sisyphus shoved his rock for eternity up
        the mountain said rock always toppled down,
                so I must daily hike my middle-aged ass

north off the back of my leg, get my pulse
        to pump or risk returning sooner to earth
                than if I didn't. My hill's a red triangle

slashed across a postcard of night—
        two red dots becoming three and so on,
                each interval a slope I sweat

to stay atop. The high window I face
        holds a netless orange hoop
                my bare-chested son tries to arc

a basketball through. My older nephew
        shouts *sweet* and *swish,* along with *airball*
                when the miss is shameless.

Nearby my white-haired mom, sunk in a web chair,
        squints at *Cloud of Unknowing,*
                a medieval text on Christian prayer

that urges self-forgetting the better
        to know God's will. In Mother's hazel eyes
                those words are real; this world is faded print;

real my father's chlorine-scented ghost in work clothes
        by the pool, while the boys who gallop past like young
                ponies don't even draw a glance. "Life's

suffering," Buddha taught, and decades ago,
        Mother lit an incense cone to ponder this.
                My stick legs wouldn't fit the yoga posture.

And when she closed her eyes to OM,
        my world went black. The cone burned down to ash.
                Now this lit console records my progress—cals

burned, miles gone, minutes till goal. Now the death
        I sweat to flee she leans into, each day
                more inward. Though her body shaped mine,

willed me into light, I now cling
        to keep her from the dark I started in,
                unknowable mist. . . . Clouds drift past the pane.

In cut-offs by the pool, my sister skims
        dragonflies and skater spiders
                with a shallow net. Tan, long-legged,

she looks sixteen, and crouches to pinch what seems
        a lime green butterfly, hand-sized, from her catch.
                Mother sleeps, book fallen, white head atilt.

The boys leap like wild stags. From my chest
        there radiates for them such a flowering
                my steps have eased. Look

how light I've grown, moonwalking
        down the easy slope, though head bent, dripping sweat.
                These stairs have mastered me.

The console's cherry-red marquee blinks END! I sink again,
      another interval logged, which earns
            but lessened gravity, a weary peace.

Now I catch a whiff of Lecia's cornbread
      with sinus-opening chile—volcanic red,
            burbling on the stove, rich with smashed garlic,

hacked onion, like Dad taught us to make.
      I can hear the old chipped plates being set,
            spigots opened to wash hands. Soon

we'll be clapped to our chairs for grace.

                    for Lecia

CHOSEN BLINDNESS

1.

I was blind to flowers for one thing.
Picture a meadow stitched with dandelion,
those seed stalks whose tall white heads

poke up like ancestral ghosts
(pale auroras of wisdom), but profligate,
the fluff shot through with brown seeds

that others might follow. I never saw it,
just fixed on my own death, sat on the sofa
ingesting poison, looked out

at the rectangular field as if it were a postcard
from some foreign land, useless, already canceled.
I sucked streams of gray smoke down my lungs

to blacken me deeper. The embroidery sampler I did in x's
read BAD NEWS. The butterless popcorn I ate
was a bowl full of spiders. Skinny?

My skeleton forced itself forward. No word
of praise passed my lips though a million breaths
moved through me. That's what human bodies do, keep

breathing, no matter the venom their brains manufacture.

2.

Now I go to church. Who'd think it?
We stand in rows, like graves, I'd once have thought,
like herd beasts lined up for slaughter. Now I notice

our bodies bend in the same places. We form the same angles.
To sing together, we have to breathe in unison,
draw the same air into the dark meat of our bodies

as if it actually were spiritu sancti and ourselves
that spirit incarnate. Every now and then,
a toddler bolts up the main aisle, pursued

by a lumbering adult. Babies list
in sloping arms and toothless grin.
The old lean on canes

and chrome walkers set down slow. People
pause to let them pass. Always a list of dead is read,
always the sick are mentioned so your own aches

seem aggressively minor. My forebears
forbore this way, in company. Bread fed them,
and they had to practice hope to keep

plowing up the Dust Bowl's
starved earth in rows, year
after fruitless year, till the cotton came back.

   3.

At the end of my drinking,
I coiled a garden hose in the back of my station wagon
and set off driving to a town

called Marblehead to breathe in the cool
exhaust and thus stop thoughts from streaming
through my mind like bad current.

I'd left my infant son a note, glowing green
on my computer screen, how he'd be
better off. Now a column of sun

through high windows shines
on his blond head. His hand
holds half our hymnal, index finger

underlining each word as we struggle
to match up our voices, hold the beat,
find the pattern emerging, feel the light

that glows in our chests, keep it going.

for Dev Milburn

AGAINST DECORATION

AGAINST DECORATION

1

Decoration abounds in contemporary poetry, much of it marching beneath the banner of neo-formalism. Actually a mix of strict form and free verse, the new formalist poems juggle rhyme, meter, and various syllabic and stanzaic strategies. In the last ten years, the movement has generated a rush of anthologies, such as Robert Richman's *The Direction of Poetry: Rhymed and Metered Verse Written in the English Language Since 1975*. Richman, the poetry editor of the neo-conservative *New Criterion*, selects not only distinguished writers such as the late James Merrill, John Hollander, and Anthony Hecht (all of whom, by the way, have served as chancellors for the Academy of American Poets), but also from the forty-something generation that includes Michael Blumenthal, Gjertrud Schnackenberg, Brad Leithauser, and Rosanna Warren. This book produced one outraged notice by poet-critic Ira Sadoff, who in an issue of *The American Poetry Review* called neo-formalism "A Dangerous Nostalgia," linking it to the political conservatism of the eighties. Once a poetry movement can boast an anthology, a starting date, and a metaphorically machine-gunning detractor, it qualifies as a movement—even if it lacks a coherent manifesto.

The fault, of course, doesn't lie with form per se. The late Amy Clampitt rarely employed strict forms, yet her work is almost exclusively ornamental, particularly in her overuse of historical references, which seem to increase in their obscurity over the course of her books. Her *Collected Poems* came out this year to vague but unanimous praise. It's easier to know what Clampitt's read than what she's writing about (the notes for *Westward* consume four-and-a-half pages). Critics have called her obscure, polysyllabic diction a long-awaited return to high language, likening her to Hopkins, Keats, and Milton. But Clampitt's purple vocabulary sounds to me like a parody of the Victorian silk that Pound sought to unravel. This passage could be Swinburne on acid or Tennyson gone mad with his thesaurus. In it, the sun is rising or setting:

Seamless equipose of crossing: Nox
primordial half-shape above the treadle,
the loomed fabric of the sun god's ardor
foreshortened, with a roar as if of earthly fire.

(from "Winchester: The Autumn Equinox")

Influential critics have cheered Clampitt's linguistic intricacy for
its own sake. And the appreciation for ornament extends to oth-
ers. In April 1990, *The New Republic* carried Helen Vendler's semi-
nal review of Merrill's *The Inner Room* beneath the telling headline
"In Praise of Perfume." There, she aligned Merrill with writers "in-
terested in intricacy of form, and a teasing obliqueness of con-
tent." In Merrill's "Losing the Marbles," Vendler enjoys a kind of
crossword puzzle challenge:

> A poem-manuscript has been rained on, and some of its
> words obliterated. On its half unreadable "papyrus," the
> poem looks like one of Sappho's enigmatic fragments:
>
>> body, favorite
>>> gleaned, at the
>>>> vital
>>>> frenzy—
>
> —and so on, for seven stanzas. The game is to deduce what
> the poem's lost cells may have been holding. . . . We be-
> come, with Merrill, scholars of the papyrus, hunters for lost
> words—and find ourselves (in a mockery of classical scholarly
> reconstructions) wholly mistaken.

There's something scary about Vendler's enthusiasm for the poem
as scholastic game, particularly when her efforts leave her "wholly
mistaken." I always thought that poetry's primary purpose was to
stir emotion, and that one's delight in dense idiom or syntax or al-
lusion served a secondary one. I don't mind, for instance, working
hard to read *Paradise Lost*, because I return to Milton for the terror

and hubris Satan embodies. If, as Vendler suggests, the sport of decoding a poem is its central pleasure, then one would no more reread such a poem than one would bother reworking an acrostic already solved. Indeed, such a poem would become disposable after one reading, the "game" played.

Yet the affection for decorative poetry extends beyond Vendler to other powerful critics, poets, and publishers: Vendler begat Clampitt and others; Harold Bloom begat John Ashbery and the poetics of coy adorableness, which in turn begat Language Poetry; Merrill begat a string of ornament-spouting progeny through his service at Yale University Press and the Academy, as well as through his general pull with New York publishers (his *blurbissimo* on book jackets was famous); Alice Quinn, poetry editor for *The New Yorker,* begat the flowery, emotionally dim poems that one typically reads in that magazine; *ad nauseam.*

The argument against decoration, however, runs as far back as literary criticism itself. Aristotle called metaphors of all kinds the mere "seasoning of the meat," and believed that clarity resided instead in "everyday words." Cicero and Horace basically elaborated this dichotomy between seasoning and substance. Ancient rhetoricians admonished writers to avoid—among other things—excessive use of tropes. These elaborate figures of speech could, it was argued, over-decorate a work and reduce its power to convey feeling. In fact, the *Princeton Encyclopedia of Poetry and Poetics* tells us that the poet and orator in the early Christian era had to justify the use of a limited number of tropes by demonstrating the extremity of his or her own feeling. In other words, unless the orator could convey the depth and sincerity of his or her own experience, the use of tropes fell into the realm of mere decoration. That's how I often feel about much of today's popular work: The poet concentrates so fixedly on the poem's minute needlework that he or she fails to notice—like a blind man with the elephant in the old fable—that the work involves only one square inch of a tapestry draped across an enormous beast, and that the beast is moving.

I define two sins popular in much of today's poetry—particularly the neo-formalist stuff—which signify decoration and can starve a poem of value:

1. *Absence of emotion.* What should I as a reader feel? This grows from but is not equivalent to what the speaker/author feels. Questioning a poem's central emotion steers me beyond the poem's ostensible subject and surface lovelinesses to its ultimate effect. Purely decorative poetry leaves me cold.

2. *Lack of clarity.* The forms of obscurity in decorative poetry are many and insidious: references that serve no clear purpose, for instance, or ornate diction that seeks to elevate a mundane experience rather than clarify a remarkable one. Lack of clarity actually alienates a reader and prevents any emotional engagement with the poem.

Again, I do not decry decorative elements in a poem per se. One can with perfect legitimacy use a reference or create an elaborately metaphoric or linguistic surface in a poem. But when those elements become final ends, rather than acting as a conduit for a range of feelings, poetry ceases to perform its primary function: to move the reader. To pay so little attention to the essentially human elements of a poem makes a monster of poetry's primary emotional self, its very reason for being, so that the art becomes exclusively decorative and at times grotesque. Like cats in jewelry or babies in makeup, the ornaments detract from rather than illuminate their subjects.

Absence of Emotion

We can marshal evidence for the emotional vacuity of ornamental verse with the example of Merrill, who may well have been the first emperor of the new formalism. I contend that this emperor wore no clothes—or, to use a more accurate metaphor, that the ornamental robes existed, but the emperor himself was always missing—a surprising state of affairs, since Merrill was among the most revered and ubiquitous poets of his generation: He boasted two National Book Awards, the Bollingen, the Pulitzer, and the National Book Critics Circle Award.

Merrill's chief talent is his mastery of elegant language. And in his earlier work, the complexity of language and metaphor applies to human dramas that are grounded enough in the world to move a reader. In "Charles on Fire," for example, we hear some privileged young men at dinner discussing the difference between "uncommon physical good looks," which are believed to "launch one," and "intellectual and spiritual values," without which "you are sunk." In this poem, Merrill gives us far more narrative data than he bothers with in his more recent books. Knowing certain physical and social facts, the reader can become sufficiently engaged in the poem to marvel at Merrill's sparing use of ornament. Here is the final two-thirds of the poem:

> Long-suffering Charles, having cooked and served the meal,
> Now brought out little tumblers finely etched
> He filled with amber liquid and then passed.
> "Say," said the same young man, "in Paris, France,
> They do it this way"—bounding to his feet
> And touching a lit match to our host's full glass.
> A blue flame, gentle, beautiful, came, went
> Above the surface. In a hush that fell
> We heard the vessel crack. The contents drained
> As who should step down from a crystal coach.
> Steward of spirits, Charles's glistening hand
> All at once gloved itself in eeriness.
> The moment passed. He made two quick sweeps and
> Was flesh again. "It couldn't matter less,"
> He said, but with a shocked, unconscious glance
> Into the mirror. Finding nothing changed,
> He filled a fresh glass and sank down among us.

Charles literally *serves,* and serves to contrast with his guests, who seem more foppish than he. In fact, Charles draws the poet's pretty diction by bringing out "little tumblers finely etched," a phrase that throws in lovely sideways relief the noise of "filled with amber liquid." This diction is juxtaposed with the poem's plain speech, something which—like narrative clarity—Merrill rarely employs in later work. At the instant the liquor catches fire, Merrill's staccato suspends us for an instant. Here's a wonderful example of a transforming moment that *requires* its adjectives and commas and one-syllable words to hold us at a key instant: "A blue flame, gentle, beautiful, came, went / Above the surface." And how convincing and surprising is the higher diction in the next lines when Charles, like Cinderella's footman "down from a crystal coach," briefly enters the realm of fire: "Steward of spirits, Charles's glistening hand / All at once gloved itself in eeriness." After this, the diction again irons out, becomes plain. "The moment passed. He made two quick sweeps and / Was flesh again. 'It couldn't matter less,' / He said. . . ." When Charles finds nothing changed about his outward appearance, he returns from the consuming to the mundane, from fire to flesh. In doing so, he literally sinks to the level of the others. Here the poet never embellishes a line with blowsy diction or froufrou unless it warrants such decor.

Parts of Merrill's later work show the old sparkle, but often the flourishes obscure the central subject, render it meaningless. Here, from *The Inner Room*, is "Serenade" *in toto:*

> Here's your letter the old portable
> Pecked out so passionately as to crack
> The larynx. I too dream of "times
> We'll share." Across the river: MUTUAL LIFE.
>
> Flush of a skyline. Owning up to past
> Decorum, present insatiety,
> Let corporate proceedings one by one
> Be abstracted to mauve onionskin,
>
> Lit stories rippling upside down in thought
> Be stilled alike of drift and personnel,
> Then, only then, the lyric I-lessness
> At nightfall banked upon renew
>
> Today's unfolder. Whose lips part. Heard now
> In his original setting—voice and reeds—
> As music for a god, your page
> Asks to be held so that the lamp shines through
>
> And stars appear instead of periods.

Merrill never clarifies the central characters in this memory, or the relation between the *you* and *I*. A serenade suggests a night song played under the balcony of the beloved. And the poem hints at tremendous feeling—the letter so passionately typed that the periods have pounded holes in the paper. But never does the poet furnish the information required by the reader to understand and, thereby, feel moved. Instead, one small question after another niggles me. I don't know who serenades whom, so I don't know whether the letter writer's larynx cracks or the reader-poet's larynx cracks. If the former, typing does not touch the larynx; if the latter, there's a sick bathos to having one's voice crack while *singing* one's own poem. I don't know what "past decorum" and "present insatiety" mean, and I very much want to, because it sounds sexual. Unfortunately, the only excerpt from the letter is as meaningless a line as can be found on any Hallmark card, "I too dream of 'times / We'll share.'" The idea and tone suggest a foggy yearning, yet the source of that yearning remains blurred. Merrill's peculiar diction, however, seizes our attention: We guess at some business association with that official-sounding language; then we slip into gushlike "lyric I-lessness / At nightfall." The final stanza seems to allude to the famous musical duel between Apollo and Marsyas (the god won, and Marsyas was flayed and nailed to a tree for his arrogance), yet the reference seems dragged in (kicking and screaming, in my opinion) solely to demonstrate the writer's erudition. I never understand any clear link between Apollo and Marsyas and the two characters in the poem, or between the poet serenading and the letter writer's star-studded letter. We guess that a parallel exists, but how does it illuminate the poem's human situation?

I can only conclude that Merrill didn't mind these obscurities of character and metaphor, which leave us to gape at the poem's gorgeous surface—the mixed diction, the clever double entendre of "MUTUAL LIFE." Indeed, this surface seems the poet's final goal. Merrill wants to dazzle us, perhaps, with his dexterity and his ability to crank out metaphors, yet he doesn't value the ostensible subject here enough to communicate narrative data about it. The subject barely merits his attention at all, acting only as a backdrop for glittery pushpins of language and metaphor.

My test for a poem's emotional clarity is this elementary exercise: Can you fill in a blank about a poem's subject with an emotional word? *The Waste Land*, for instance, is a poem about spiritual despair. It is also about lots of ideas, not least of which is a twentieth-century decay of faith which precipitates that despair. But it strives to create that despair in the reader. That's why I return to it, not to test my knowledge of Greek myth and the Upanishads (references to which I had to look up initially anyway), but to rediscover the gravity of certain ideas with the conviction that is only born of feeling.

In my view, emotion in a reader derives from reception of a clear rendering of primal human experiences: fear of death, desire, loss of love, celebration of being. To spark emotion, a poet must strive to attain what Aristotle called simple clarity. The world that the reader apprehends through his or her senses must be clearly painted, even if that world is wholly imaginary, as, say, in much of the work of Wallace Stevens.

In Merrill's later poems, intricate surface and form seem like mere amusements, rather than paths to or from human experience. Such decoration cuts a great gulf between form and meaning, with form favored over an attempt to communicate, word divorced from world, a kind of brittle cleverness supplanting emotion, wit elevated above clarity.

Contrast Merrill's poetry with that of Seamus Heaney, who works in form and still attends scrupulously to the human and sensory data that ultimately prompt emotion. Heaney proves, as do centuries of formal verse, that form and ornament do not in and of themselves diminish a poem's emotional possibilities. He never lets linguistic loveliness or metaphoric surface deter him from the primary task of inspiring feeling, nor does he seek to mystify facts by draping them in veil after veil of metaphor. The metaphoric and linguistic prettinesses balance somehow; they seem carefully chosen to move us. Heaney's sonnet sequence about his mother's death, in *The Haw Lantern,* elegantly and economically sends us all the sensory and social information we need to enter the poem's world. Here is the third sonnet from "Clearances":

When all the others were away at Mass
I was all hers as we peeled potatoes.
They broke the silence, let fall one by one
Like solder weeping off the soldering iron:
Cold comforts set between us, things to share
Gleaming in a bucket of clean water.
And again let fall. Little pleasant splashes
From each other's work would bring us to our senses.

So while the parish priest at her bedside
Went hammer and tongs at the prayers for the dying
And some were responding and some crying
I remembered her head bent towards my head,
Her breath in mine, our fluent dipping knives—
Never closer the whole rest of our lives.

Heaney begins the poem with gentle end rhymes, sometimes settling for mere consonance—*Mass* and *potatoes, one* and *iron, share* and *water, bedside* and *head.* He doesn't hit the reader on the skull with the form at first. Like Shakespeare, who endlessly varied his iambic pentameter, Heaney doesn't want the poem's noise to weigh too heavily on the ear and risk obliterating the more colloquial noises, for the poem consists of natural speech: The priest "*went* hammer and tongs at the prayers for the dying."

But after the volta—that space between the big stanza and the small one that traditionally marks a turn in the sonnet—Heaney moves to the present reality, his mother's deathbed, where he remembers their intimacy over the chore of peeling potatoes. Here the meter strengthens, becomes more regular, more heavily stressed. In doing so, it gathers force. The image of the two heads bent toward each other as they peel potatoes, forever near yet forever apart, like saints in stained glass, is luminous. "Her breath in mine" is also touching: on first reading because of the physical closeness that the two almost choose to ignore by tending to their chore; on second reading because we realize that she shared her breath with him *in utero,* then lost that breath on her deathbed. Yes, the dipping knives are adjectivally "fluent," and thereby reminiscent of speech, but the resulting metaphor—fluent, expressive silence—neither distracts from nor conflicts with the human drama under study. Rather the metaphor *enhances.* The bucket of water subtly conjures both holy water and the life-giving fluid of the womb—the waters that cleanse us and slosh us forth into the world. The fluency of the knives echoes the way music—in this case potato peels weeping from a knife into water—"bring[s] us to our senses." By the remembered sound of the water, the poet re-creates in us that rare intimacy. And Heaney has no trouble making a direct statement of feeling at poem's end. Whereas Merrill would cling to emotional obliquity, Heaney earns the right to the weighty yet musical directness of his last line: "Never closer the whole rest of our lives."

Lack of Clarity

All too many contemporary poems, particularly those in the burgeoning neo-formalist canon, shy away from passion. For example, the vast majority of *New Yorker* poems favor botanical subjects, and seldom travel any farther than the poet's flower bed. Or when poets pretend to more earnest topics, the formal elements—mere surface, the pattern in the lace, if you will—replace emotional, rhetorical, and sensory clarity. The forms of obscurity are many and insidious. I set forth the following list of those that bothered me when reading Richman's anthology:

> 1. *Obscurity of character.* Who is speaking to whom and why? What relation do the characters in the poem hold to each other? How should the reader perceive them? Even in poems that assume the intimate tone of direct speech, with the reader as eavesdropper, I seldom—in the work of Merrill or Leithauser, say—understand the relationship between the characters, or even their identities in the most prosaic sense. Are they male or female; friends, lovers, or relatives; intimates, strangers; etc.?

2. *Foggy physical world.* Where are we, and why does the poem occur here rather than elsewhere? Often physical reality remains so out of focus, with shifts in locale merely used for shifts in tone, that it's likely that the reader will be baffled. Again, I invoke Stevens's work to exemplify a wildly imagined series of overlapping places, yet each rendered precisely and appropriately.

3. *Overuse of meaningless references.* Many contemporary poets insert perplexingly obscure literary, historical, and artistic allusions, seemingly to impress us with their cleverness and sophistication.

4. *Metaphors that obscure rather than illuminate.* I. A. Richards distinguished between the metaphoric tenor (the thing actually under discussion, e.g., love in "My love is a red, red rose") and the vehicle (the rose in the aforementioned metaphor). In decorative poetry the vehicle may stand clear—the star-studded letter, for instance, in Merrill's "Serenade"—but the tenor stays out of focus, or the relation between tenor and vehicle cannot be deduced. In fact, many poets fling their metaphors (including similes, synecdoches, etc.) about like so many rhinestones, simply to change tone and, therefore, to muddle key facts.

5. *Linguistic excess for no good reason.* Polysyllables, archaic language, intricate syntax, yards of adjectives—these linguistic ornaments will slow a reader. Sometimes this needs to happen. In "Charles on Fire," for example, the change in language used to describe a transforming moment works a kind of magic, one that *should* command our attention. Look, Merrill says, this person's world is changing. On the other hand, when Clampitt spends five lines saying that the sun rose or set while Keats took a walk, one wonders why she stopped at five. Why not six, or thirty-six?

Richman's anthology proves that a younger generation of writers has followed Merrill's lead in terms of ornament and obscurity. In Michael Blumenthal's "Inventors," the metaphor serves to decorate a startlingly banal experience:

> "Imagine being the first to say: *surveillance,*"
> the mouth taking in air like a swimmer, the tongue
> light as an astronaut, gliding across the roof
> of the mouth, the eyes burning like the eyes of Fleming
> looking at mold and thinking: *penicillin.*

Blumenthal uses metaphor the way certain bad cooks use garlic and oregano. He mixes "swimmer" with "astronaut" with "Fleming" with "mouth," all to describe something finally trivial. And Rosanna Warren's "History as Decoration" provides an even more meaningless text in an idiom that sounds Victorian. In a very short space, Warren commits every decorative crime I could imagine:

> Float over us, Florence, your banners
> of assassination, your most expensive
> reds: Brazil, Majorca, lichen, cochineal.
> Let the Neoplatonic Arno flow
> crocus yellow. Let palazzo walls
> flaunt quattrocentro dyes: "little
> monk" and "lion skin." We pay for beauty; beautiful
> are gorgeous crimes we cannot feel—
>
> they shone long ago. And those philosophies
> too pretty in spirit ever to be real.
> City of fashion, Leonardo chose
> the hanged Pazzi conspirator for a theme . . .

This sounds like an art history student, perhaps in a seminar entitled "Pigment and the Florentine Imagination," rushing to answer a very long essay question to which we as readers were not privy. I cannot even say what this seeks to describe. Nor can I imagine the origin of the quotes, what this has to do with Leonardo, or how any river—even the Arno—can be Neoplatonic. Not all the poems in Richman's anthology are this bad, but I reserve the right, having plowed assiduously through fields of this kind of drivel, to choose the worst examples to make any point. If this is poetry, let us write prose.

2

Some Isms behind the Ornaments:

Some powerful "isms" lurk behind the current rage for ornamental poetry: neo-formalism I've mentioned, but I also want to consider the symbolist tolerance for obscurity, as well as the role of academic critics, who not only seem happy to take on the decorative poet's communicative burden, but whose post-structuralist theories have undermined the value of poetic clarity.

Since I've already taken a swipe at neo-formalism, I would like to start with it. I don't propose here to gauge the virtues or vices inherent in poetic forms. I agree with Coleridge when he described meter as the "yeast, worthless and disagreeable by itself . . . but giving vivacity and spirit to the liquor with which it is proportionately combined." The key word here is *proportionately*, suggesting a need to balance formal concerns with others. Good poems, in fact, always assume the precise forms required. In truth, both meaning and feeling reside in sound. As a student, I read Walter Pater's famous injunction: "All art constantly aspires towards the condition of music," which I took to mean that form in poetry should finally be indistinguishable from content in the best work. A particular musical pitch in itself refers to no *thing* in the physical world, yet when we hear it in Schumann, it evokes a feeling in relation to the notes that come before and after it, so that it means something different in one concerto than in another.

So for me, sound always means something. Yeats haunts us when he writes that the heroes of the quelled Irish rebellion are not just dead but "are changed, changed utterly: / A terrible beauty is born." Here's the roll call of heroes from that famous final stanza:

I write it out in a verse—
MacDonagh and MacBride
And Connolly and Pearse
Now and in time to be,
Wherever green is worn,
Are changed, changed utterly:
A terrible beauty is born.

(from "Easter 1916")

These brief lines, like all good ones, prove the veracity of their form. Yeats plants the names in our minds with the pounding sound he's used throughout the poem. Then he challenges that expectation by varying the stanza's pattern of stresses. The caesura buried in the penultimate line lends force to the repeated word "changed": "are *changed, changed ut*terly:" The form of the line climbs toward the three stresses in the middle; the peak even holds an extra instant because of the comma. The peak then slides to unstressed syllables at the line's end. The sound mirrors, in a way, the revolutionary insurgence and decline of the heroes killed in the 1916 Irish rebellion. The final three-beat iambic line, however, arrives with a different noise, in part because of what's preceded it. Whereas the penultimate line peaked and then sagged, the final line hammers home Yeats's point with a tragic-sounding, dirge-like beat: "a *ter*rible *beau*ty is *born.*" The last word rings with the reverberating "n" sound like a gong being struck. The sound *is* the meaning. It's nearly impossible to imagine altering a syllable of this without ruining it.

One would think, then, that anyone who delighted in traditional formal verse (I do) would welcome the new, unless, as in Sadoff's case, you think that neo-formalism posits some offensive social agenda (I don't).

And a few of the poems in Richman's anthology—particularly the light verse pieces—work. Anthony Hecht's "The Ghost in the Martini" uses the same ironic diction I love in Larkin to render an elder poet seducing or being seduced by a literary groupie. Who can fail to be amused by the first stanza:

> Over the rim of the glass
> Containing a good martini with a twist
> I eye her bosom and consider a pass,
> Certain we'd not be missed
>
> In the general hubbub. . . .

The trouble with this kind of light verse, however successful, is that, like *lite* beer and *lite* salad dressing, it leaves one hungry for something more substantial. Hecht's poem may echo bouncingly through my head the next time a visiting writer swoops an attractive student away to the nearest Motel 6, but such poems do not achieve the grandeur that, say, the last section of Stevens's "Esthétique du Mal" does—a grandeur of music and meaning as well as of form.

> The greatest poverty is not to live
> In a physical world, to feel that one's desire
> Is too difficult to tell from despair. Perhaps,
> After death, the non-physical people, in paradise,
> Itself non-physical, may, by chance, observe
> The green corn gleaming and experience
> The minor of what we feel. . . .

Once I read those lines, they returned and altered my perceptions. And they returned frequently. In fact, there have been whole years of my life during which, on a daily basis, I needed to imagine that the non-physical people, these blank-faced angels—whom I think of, because of Stevens's wonderful phrasing, as a string of slightly depressed clerical workers waiting for a subway—looked down and envied in me the very passions that caused me difficulty. Hecht's poem states a social and anecdotal truth of a lower order than the great emotional or metaphysical truths that can change one's life.

In unhappy fact, most of the people who embrace neo-formalism and are most closely identified with it (Merrill and Leithauser, say, rather than Kunitz) seem, unlike their putative ancestors (Keats, say), to see formal excellence as an aesthetic virtue in and of itself, betraying little emotional intention.

That said, let me iterate Richman's noble-sounding call for a revival of form. He says that neo-formalism will free us from ". . . two decades of obscure, linguistically flat poetry." In place of this grim stuff, Richman offers poems with the "sheer sensuous appeal of language." Only the most stiff-necked Anglo-Saxon farmer might shy away from the Francophile seduction of the phrase "sheer sensuous appeal"—it almost sounds like an ad for pantyhose. But behind Richman's seductive promise lurks a hoary dichotomy—linguistically flat poetry versus linguistically ornate verse. This dichotomy originates in part from a conflict in American poetry between free verse and formal.

In our memories, the free-verse advocates sought—among other things—to iron the aristocratic curlicues from poetic diction in order to make poetry sound more populist, less elitist, and, therefore, more American. Ralph Waldo Emerson first called for a purely American poet, and Whitman answered. The poets I think of as belonging to this free-verse lineage are Ezra Pound, William Carlos Williams, the Lowell of *Life Studies,* the Beats à la Allen Ginsberg with his jangling finger cymbals, the Black Mountain poets (in particular Robert Creeley), the Naked Poets of the famous anthology (Robert Bly, James Wright, Denise Levertov, *et al.*), and African-American poets (such as Langston Hughes and Gwendolyn Brooks). Common wisdom holds that the free-verse revolution in this country only follows the same path as other formal changes through history. But the revolution has not so much opposed strict form as strict form *and* a certain kind of idiom. Timothy Steele explains it best in *Missing Measures: Modern Poetry and the Revolt Against Meter,* claiming that the modern revolution

> differed from the revolution Euripedes led against Aeschylean style and the revolution Horace led against the literary conservatism of the day; and it differed from—to refer to Eliot's favorite examples—the revolution which Dryden led against Cleveland and the metaphysicals and the revolution which Wordsworth led against the Augustans. . . . The Modern movement's leaders . . . identified the Victorian diction against which they were rebelling (and the subject matter associated with the diction) with metrical composi-

tion *per se.* Having made this identification, they felt that to dispose of objectionable Victorian idiom, they had to dispose of meter.

Shortly after the turn of the century, Steele goes on to note, T. E. Hulme equated meter with both rhetoric and stylistic excesses. And it was such meter that most annoyed Pound in the Victorians, and from which he catapulted into free verse.

It's no surprise then that by the late 1970s, when I went to school, free verse and plain diction came to predominate in the M.F.A. worksheets. When Donald Hall claims in an essay that the burgeoning number of M.F.A. programs produces something called "McPoem," we who read little magazines know intuitively what he means—tone ironic, diction flat. And McPoem comes, I think, from the revolution against meter, rhetoric, and the stylistic gush that characterized the Victorian idiom. I can no more defend this line of free versers than I would seek to weigh the virtues of its form-producing siblings. I do think, however, that it's McPoem that Richman and many of the neo-formalists seek to overthrow.

And of course, there's a long and venerable tradition in America of working in meter. We think of them as sentimental and comically ornate now, but Edna St. Vincent Millay and Henry Wadsworth Longfellow used to be poetic monuments. Nor would anyone disagree that however innovative Emily Dickinson was, she drank deeply from the English wellspring. As final testimony to the powers of formal poetry, I contend that most readers can quote, if nothing else, a smidgen of Robert Frost—perhaps *the* formal poet in this century most adept at infusing measured lines and stanzas with colloquial diction, thereby satisfying both the formalists and the free versers.

Another tradition, though, that inspires much of new poetry's obliquity and lack of understandable feeling is the French symbolist tradition as it migrated here through Yeats and the High Moderns—Eliot and Stevens. Without rehashing the entire symbolist manifesto, we can say that it often suggested that poetry was, in moral and practical terms, somewhat useless. In positing this fundamental irrelevance, the symbolist idea of "art for art's sake" (Théophile Gautier's term) freed poets from many of the moral and religious imperatives that possessed, say, Milton, and haunted artists as late as the nineteenth century. It was then that John Ruskin's book *Modern Painters* held aesthetic sway. There Ruskin at one point complains that a certain painter inaccurately depicted the shape of leaves on a certain type of tree, an inaccuracy that violated painting's moral obligation to mimic the natural world. We find this notion laughable today in part because of the symbolist influence, which hinted—at times even screamed—that poetry was a purely linguistic rather than human or (to use a positivist term) synthetic experience. In fact, in this country, most formal—as opposed to moral or humanistic—criteria for judging poetry have grown directly from symbolist sources. From Rimbaud's position that poetry resulted from "a deliberate disordering of the senses," to Mallarmé's call for "pure" poetry, to Verlaine's desire to "wring the neck of rhetoric" (again, rhetoric being subtly linked in this country with Victorian excesses), the symbolists suggested that poetry needn't make much sense in terms of rational or sensory experience.

I'm saying several things with this broad characterization of recent poetic history. First, as we all know, it's not news that poets write in form. Second, neither is it news that the pendulum has swung back toward form at this particular bend in history, after several decades of increasingly plain diction. Third, while our symbolist heirs freed poetry from moral agendas, they also permitted writers not to worry much about speaking clearly (in the rhetorical and synthetic senses) to a reader.

Finally, the trend toward ornament also mirrors the end of the last century. Back then, we could also see the verse growing purpler. Like most of the pre-Raphaelites, Swinburne was a champion embellisher: Hugh Kenner slyly notes in *The Pound Era* that Swinburne once translated a single line of Sappho into eight lines of "slow-motion re-enactment." The Victorians not only embroidered language, but they managed to sentimentalize almost every subject, and to grow increasingly stern and corseted as the century drew to a close, as if anticipating the revolution in morals (prompted by Freud's *Interpretation of Dreams*) after 1900. Poets seemed to lurch away from the new century's uncertainty by looking to the art's historical roots, honoring Greek and Latin antiquities; as a way of keeping the old cultural flame alive, lots of poets sprinkled their work with heavy references. Robert Hass, who was one teacher I had in graduate school, urged me to read Browning's "Sordello"—an incredibly muddled wad of nonsense about the jongleur who brought the Provençal lyric to France—in part so I might understand why Pound roared so loudly against the Victorians. Even Pound, himself anthologized as a Victorian, grumbled that you needed to learn some dozen different languages (including five dead ones) in order to read poetry. So we see at the end of the last century a reactionary lunge back toward our poetic roots, and that lunge produced some perfectly respectable results.

Sadly, the only thing that *is* news about neo-formalism is bad news. Rarely before has form been championed as a virtue in and of itself, and poems judged formally good that in fact lack any relevance to human experience. Many of the poems in Richman's anthology seem like the husks of poems, forms with the life bled out, the assumption being that impeccably rhymed and metered verse will be good regardless of poetic content, or lack thereof. This new passion for prettiness opposes, I think, the huge body of formal work that values form only as a *relative* quality. By relative, I mean that in the past the poet asked, what kind of sound will best communicate my meaning, and vice versa. So while I defend formal verse and approve neo-formalist goals—a revival of rich language and a literary history all but ignored since the free-verse revolution—I abhor its current practice as the source of perhaps the most emotionally vacant work ever written. Moreover, the acceptance of that work has given unearned praise and canon status to writers such as Clampitt who work outside strict forms, but still homestead the realm of ornament.

Despite my wince at the assembling neo-formalist canon, I believe strongly that we as readers should not scapegoat the innocent, though Sadoff's essay in *The American Poetry Review* blames political conservatism, warning readers that

> neo-formalists have a social as well as a linguistic agenda. When they link pseudo-populism ("the general reader") to regular meter, they disguise their nostalgia for moral and linguistic certainty, for a universal ("everyone agrees") and univocal way of conserving culture.

Although I suppose that, politically speaking, I stand beside Sadoff far left of center, his approach seems misconceived. His use of the word "agenda" implies a political conspiracy. And his tone almost makes me nostalgic for the political conviction (bordering on paranoia) that was the appropriate response to the evil figures of the Watergate era. While I don't doubt that Richard Nixon conspired with his pals to lower the quality of our lives, I do doubt that Merrill did, or Vendler does. When Sadoff applies this sanctimonious tone to a reading of a Merrill poem, I doubt his sociopolitical conclusions.

> One cannot read a poem like James Merrill's "Clearing the Title" . . . and admire his fluent iambic pentameter, his complicated rhyme scheme, without acknowledging that the culminating experience of this poem involves the wealthy narrator sharing a beautiful sunset with a native "black girl with shaved skull." This "transcendent" moment allows him to make a commitment to his lover, to buy—I swear—a condo in Key West. The inherent racism of the poem . . . points out the dangers of an esthetic that ignores what is seen in favor of the pure beauty of sound.

One can discern in Sadoff's reading the same dichotomy that Richman mentioned—word versus world. Sadoff's gloss also harks back to the massive body of moral criticism after Plato. We should not, I think, look to poets or their poems for moral or political guidance, because, quite frankly, they seem to behave badly at least as often as they behave well—Larkin's misogyny and Pound's anti-Semitism pose just two examples of moral irresponsibility in our century. Nor can we as readers judge, as Sadoff tries to do, Merrill's "privileged personal stand and his obvious ambivalence toward intimacy. . . ." Who isn't ambivalent about intimacy? And how many of us writing poetry in this country aren't privileged? Moreover, the artist judged as *amoral* in his or her time—William Burroughs or Oscar Wilde, for instance—usually just proposes an unconventional moral code.

However, at a time when our eviscerated national arts program must battle censors for its very life, when rap records are stripped from shelves (No, I don't like "Slap My Bitch Up" either, but I wouldn't ban it), we must take care with our moral outrage. The key argument is not, as Sadoff implies, a political one between a free-verse liberalism and a formalist conservatism. In fact, to all moral critics I suggest reading Graham Hough, who makes these distinctions between moral- and formal-based criticism:

> It is quite possible to hold a formal theory and to hold also that literature should be subject to external control. . . . All that is necessary to form a formal theory is to hold that these moral controls *are* external and do not affect literary value. . . . [But] formal theories developed in isolation reduce literature to insignificance. Moral theories developed in isolation cease to be literary theories and become contributions to the social hygiene.

So if we can't blame form, or history, or a certain political or social position for decorative poetry, whom can we blame? I suggest that we blame criticism, so long as we're careful not to blame critics, for we still live, as Randall Jarrell told us back in the fifties, in the age of criticism. An inevitable consequence is that poets expect a critic to stand between the text and the reader.

Moreover, a new atmosphere of interplay between literary theory and poetic practice bears some responsibility. It's not hard to see the American rage for post-structuralist models of reading as furnishing covert manifestos for such poetries of surface as, say, Brad Leithauser's, much in the same way that the last century's social-Darwinist craze informed the naturalist movement in American fiction.

But unfortunately, poets tend to translate theoretical models into recipes for instant production. So post-structuralist theories about engagement with a text have frequently, I think, been misinterpreted by American avant-garde writers as a passport to fashionable literary chaos. Laypeople (like me) probably view a theoretician like Jacques Derrida as engaged in a creatively destructive enterprise—specifically, overturning post-Platonic separations between form and content, word and referent, in order to clear ground for new kinds of work. But in practice, working poets only receive Derrida's complex set of messages filtered obliquely through, say, articles in *The New York Review of Books*. Seldom can poets see past post-structuralism's dense surface of wordplay and a broad edict that the world itself is but text. Derrida's style, then, has probably had more effect than any of his theories, which are virtually indecipherable to most of us. In this way, post-structuralism endorses an over-baroque surface that's heavily allusive and unconcerned with communication.

Furthermore, if the world itself is but text, then—or so some writers mistakenly feel—that text is doomed to be a private one, a hermetic one. Again, the liberating symbolist protest against artistic conformity to social and religious mores has perhaps transformed obscurity from something to be tolerated occasionally in a poem into something required to prove the poet's seriousness. I think of Valéry's remark that symbolist poetry after Baudelaire wanted only to "tease the bourgeois reader with difficulty." Since that injunction, the poet has learned to count on the critic to clarify any message, no matter how deeply buried. Harold Bloom stands at the ready to whisper myth and meaning into the reader's ear, and to justify said reference while scaring the hell out of the average reader with words like *historicize*. Rudolph Arnheim once warned against an art that generates chaotic forms under the guise of reflecting a chaotic world. It's that very chaos that I see in the ascendancy in much decorative poetry.

With a slight nod of culpability to Derrida and de Man, *et al.,* none of whom I much understand, I do not hold deconstruction at fault in the decorative mishmash of contemporary poetry, any more than I would blame modernism for the literary confusion prompted by *The Waste Land.* But a fair measure of a theory's power is its breadth of influence, and a broad influence is doomed, in part, to be a shallow one. Deconstruction has permitted poets to be weak communicators. I'm thinking specifically of the glib meaninglessness in poets like Ashbery and his heirs, the Language Poets. It's ironic, though, that theories invented to collapse distinctions between form and content now provide writers with permission to ignore the referents of words, thereby elevating form to a communicative end in itself. As deconstructionist theories have begun blurrily appearing on our inner TV screens—part of the current *Zeitgeist*—poets have begun generating a kind of literary rubble, which cannot be built upon.

I would refute ornamental poetry—represented most obviously by the neo-formalists—on aesthetic, rather than theoretical, political, or social grounds. What I posit, and indeed, what Horace posited back in the first century B.C., is that poetry should be *dulce et util:* it should be sweet and useful, should delight and instruct; the linguistic and decorative experience of a poem should not outweigh the human or synthetic meanings.

We have collectively bemoaned how poetry's audience has dwindled to a tiny coterie, whose favor poets buy with a kind of literary jewelry. No one was wiser (or more wise-assed) about that shrinking audience than Jarrell, who wrote this almost fifty years before poetry reached the decorative zenith it holds today:

> That the poetry of the first half of this century often *was* too difficult . . . is a truism that it would be absurd to deny. How our poetry got this way—how romanticism was purified and exaggerated and "corrected" into modernism . . . how poet and public stared at each other with righteous indignation, till the poet said, "Since you won't read me, I'll make sure you can't"—is one of the most complicated and interesting of stories.

Complicated the story still is, but I wonder if Jarrell would find the highbrow doily-making that passes for art today interesting. I scarcely do, except in the way that an exorcist might find certain demons interesting.

My opinion of ornament became cemented ten years back when I sat through a partial reading of Merrill's epic *Changing Light at Sandover* at Harvard. At the crowded reception after, I stood elbow to elbow with some friends—poets and critics whose opinions I respect and who were jubilant about the performance. I asked each in turn what he or she liked in the reading, which parts were moving, because I assumed that I had *missed* something. But their faces remained empty. No one seemed to remember much. Maybe my question seemed too bone-headed to warrant an answer, but no one seized upon an instant or quoted a line to support the consensus that the reading was a smash. Yet here stood, in my opinion, a fairly elite audience. I had heard these friends in the wee hours quote Hopkins by the yard, or rehash the details of Sir Philip Sidney's *Defence of Poetry*. Yet ten minutes after an allegedly brilliant reading, the poems had merely washed past the audience, leaving no traces except for some vague murmurings.

I drove home feeling awful, thinking that something terrible had happened to poetry, that a trick had been played on readers, and small wonder that the number of readers continued to decline. Somehow, the poetry that made our pulses race, that could flood us with conviction and alter our lives, had been replaced by decoration, which can only leave us nodding smugly to one another, as if privy to some inside joke.

NOTES

"The Wife of Jesus Speaks": There's no definitive historical evidence that Jesus had a wife (or didn't). This poem dares only to speculate.

"The Last of the Brooding Miserables": When I remember James Laughlin, I think of this tombstone inscription from Larry McMurtry's *Lonesome Dove:* "Cheerful in all weathers. Never shirked a task. Splendid behavior."

"The Pallbearer": John Engman died suddenly of a cerebral hemmorrhage in 1996. His poems reward study.

"Christ's Passion": Walt Mink was not a Christian, though his life and work exemplify values that theology esteems. As professor and friend, he is sorely missed.

INDEX OF TITLES & FIRST LINES

Grateful acknowledgment is made to all those who gave permission to reprint in the essay "Against Decoration" quoted material from previously published sources: an excerpt from "Inventors" from *Sympathetic Magic* by Michael Blumenthal (Copyright © 1980 by Michael Blumenthal), reprinted by permission of the author; "Winchester: The Autumn Equinox" from *The Collected Poems of Amy Clampitt* by Amy Clampitt (Copyright © 1997 by The Estate of Amy Clampitt), reprinted by permission of Alfred A. Knopf, Inc.; an excerpt from "Clearances" from *The Haw Lantern* by Seamus Heaney (Copyright © 1987 by Seamus Heaney), reprinted by permission of Farrar, Straus & Giroux, Inc.; "The Ghost in the Martini" from *Collected Earlier Poems* by Anthony Hecht (Copyright © 1990 by Anthony Hecht), reprinted by permission of Alfred A. Knopf, Inc.; "Essay on Criticism" by Graham Hough from *The Selected Essays* (Copyright © 1978 by Graham Hough), reprinted by permission of Cambridge University Press, Inc.; an excerpt from *Poetry and the Age* by Randall Jarrell (Copyright © 1980 by Randall Jarrell), reprinted by permission of The Estate of Randall Jarrell; "Charles on Fire" by James Merrill from *Selected Poems 1946-1988* by James Merrill (Copyright © 1992 by James Merrill), reprinted by permission of Alfred A. Knopf, Inc.; "Serenade" from *The Inner Room* by James Merrill (Copyright © 1988 by James Merrill), reprinted by permission of Alfred A. Knopf; an excerpt from *Missing Measures: Modern Poetry and the Revolt Against Meter* by Timothy Steele (Copyright © 1990 by Timothy Steele), reprinted by permission of the University of Arkansas Press; "Esthetique du Mal" from the *Collected Poems* by Wallace Stevens (Copyright 1947 by Wallace Stevens), reprinted by permission of Alfred A. Knopf, Inc.; "History as Decoration" from *Each Leaf Shines Separate* by Rosanna Warren (Copyright © 1984 by Rosanna Warren), reprinted by permission of W.W. Norton, Inc.

Mary Karr's poems and criticism have appeared in *Parnassus, The Atlantic Monthly, Poetry, The American Poetry Review, The Harvard Review, The New Yorker, The New York Times Magazine,* and others. Her first collection was *Abacus* (Wesleyan University Press, 1987) and her second *The Devil's Tour* (New Directions, 1993). She received a Bunting fellowship from Radcliffe College and a Whiting Writers Award, as well as two Pushcart prizes (poetry and essay) and the Tietjins Award from *Poetry.* Other grants include the NEA and state funds from Minnesota and Massachusetts. Her bestselling memoir *The Liars' Club* won the PEN Martha Albrand Award for first nonfiction, The Texas Institute of Letters Prize for nonfiction, and was a finalist for The National Book Critics Circle Award. It was excerpted in *Esquire* and *Granta,* and was chosen as one of the best books of 1995 by over one hundred newspapers and magazines. She has taught poetry and literature at Tufts, Harvard, Sarah Lawrence, and Syracuse University.